SAYINGS
OF MAO OF JESUS

DICK HILLIS, Editor

A Division of G/L Publications
Glendale, California, U.S.A.

Scripture quotations from the **New American Standard Bible,** copyright 1971 by The Lockman Foundation, La Habra, California. Used by permission.

Second Printing, 1972.

© Copyright 1972 by G/L Publications, Glendale, California 91209.
All rights reserved.
Printed in U.S.A.

Published by Regal Books Division, G/L Publications
Glendale, California 91209

Library of Congress Catalog Card No. 71-178099
ISBN 0-8307-0141-9

FOREWORD

Today the sayings of Jesus Christ, the man of
Galilee, are bywords in the Western world.
In the vast mainland of China, the sayings of
Chairman Mao Tse-Tung are holy writ to nearly
800 million people.

I am a child of both of these cultures, the
Chinese and the American. I am an American
by birth and a Chinese by adoption, having
married and raised a family in China.

In 1971-72 the Chinese Communist Party
celebrates its half-century anniversary while
the United States is being swept by the Jesus
revolution. What do Mao and Jesus have to
say about the issues confronting us today?
Are they in agreement on any issue? What
are their goals?

I have personally indulged in what has been
an exciting philosophical project — contrasting
the ideologies expressed in their writings. Now
in this book I am inviting the thoughtful
reader to consider and compare the sayings
of Mao and Jesus.

94960

Mao looks to the masses for the creative forces for betterment. Jesus stresses need for individual response to the dynamic of his deity and person. The reader will discover, as we did, that no one is able to embrace simultaneously the doctrines of both.

Mao's sayings may sound to some like Marxist-Leninist abstractions, but they are intended as exhortations designed to create dedicated world revolutionaries. Jesus' statements may sound like the simplistic directives of an elightened rabbi, but their credence lies squarely on his claim to deity. Both Mao and Jesus knew the discipline of toil. Both appeal to the common man.

I am indebted to my friend Norman Rohrer for his assistance in excerpting these contrasting sayings, the distillation of teachings by two revolutionaries.

Dick Hillis

5

"Our country and all the other socialist countries want peace; so do the peoples of all the countries of the world."

MAO

Opening Address at the Eighth National Congress of the Communist Party of China (September 15, 1956).

"We take up swords, too, following his (Chiang Kai-shek's) example . . . As Chiang Kai-shek is now sharpening his swords, we must sharpen ours too."

MAO

The Situation and Our Policy after the Victory in the War of Resistance Against Japan (August 13, 1945), **Selected Works,** Vol. IV, pp. 14-15.

"Peace I leave with you; My peace I give to you; not as the world gives, do I give to you."

JESUS

John 14:27

"Put your sword back into its place; for all those who take up the sword shall perish by the sword."

JESUS

Matthew 26:52

"War is the highest form of struggle for resolving contradictions, when they have developed to a certain stage, between classes, nations, states, or political groups, and it has existed ever since the emergence of private property and of classes."

MAO

Problems of Strategy in China's Revolutionary War (December 1936), **Selected Works,** Vol. I, p. 180.

"Blessed are the peacemakers, for they shall be called sons of God."

JESUS

Matthew 5:9

"Politics is war without bloodshed while war is politics with bloodshed."

MAO

On Protracted War (May 1938),
Selected Works, Vol. II, pp. 152-53.

"What king, when he sets out to meet another king in battle, will not first sit down and take counsel whether he is strong enough with ten thousand men to encounter the one coming against him with twenty thousand?"

JESUS

Luke 14:31

"Political work is the lifeblood of all economic work."

MAO

Introductory note to a Serious Lesson (1955), **The Socialist Upsurge in China's Countryside,** Chinese ed., Vol. I.

"Render to Caesar the things that are Caesar's, and to God the things that are God's."

JESUS

Luke 20:25

"Every Communist must grasp the truth, 'Political power grows out of the barrel of a gun.'"

MAO

Problems of War and Strategy (November 6, 1938), **Selected Works,** Vol. II, p. 224.

"All authority has been given to Me in heaven and on earth."

JESUS

Matthew 28:18

"We are advocates of the omnipotence of revolutionary war; that is good, not bad, it is Marxist."

MAO

Problems of War and Strategy
(November 6, 1938), **Selected Works,**
Vol. II, p. 225.

"Whoever then humbles himself as this child, he is the greatest in the kingdom of heaven."

JESUS

Matthew 18:4

"The ultimate aim for which all communists strive is to bring about a socialist and communist society."

MAO

The Chinese Revolution and the Chinese Communist Party (December 1939), **Selected Works,** Vol. II, pp. 330-31.

"What does it profit a man to gain the whole world, and forfeit his soul?"

JESUS

Mark 8:36

"The Marxist philosophy . . . openly
avows that dialectical materialism is
in the service of the proletariat . . .
It emphasizes the dependence of
theory on practice, emphasizes that
theory is based on practice and in
turn serves practice."

MAO

On Practice (July 1937), **Selected Works,**
Vol. I, p. 297.

"You shall love the Lord your God with all your heart, and with all your soul, and with all your mind. You shall love your neighbor as yourself."

JESUS

Matthew 22:37, 39

"According to the Marxist theory of the state, the army is the chief component of state power. Whoever wants to seize and retain state power must have a strong army."

MAO

Problems of War and Strategy
(November 6, 1938), **Selected Works,**
Vol. II, p. 225.

*"My kingdom is not of this world.
If My kingdom were of this world,
then My servants would be fighting."*

JESUS

John 18:36

"Only with guns can the whole world be transformed."

MAO

Problems of War and Strategy (November 6, 1938), **Selected Works,** Vol. II, p. 225.

"I have overcome the world."

JESUS

John 16:33

"We are advocates of the abolition of war, we do not want war; but war can only be abolished through war, and in order to get rid of the gun it is necessary to take up the gun."

MAO

Problems of War and Strategy (November 6, 1938), **Selected Works,** Vol. II, p. 225.

"You have heard that it was said, 'An eye for an eye, and a tooth for a tooth.' But I say to you, do not resist him who is evil; but whoever slaps you on your right cheek, turn to him the other also."

JESUS

Matthew 5:38,39

"War, this monster of mutual slaughter among men, will be finally eliminated by the progress of human society, and in the not too distant future too. But there is only one way to eliminate it and that is to oppose war with war."

MAO

Problems of Strategy in China's Revolutionary War (December 1936), **Selected Works,** Vol. I, pp. 182-83.

"Nation will rise against nation, and kingdom against kingdom, and in various places there will be famines and earthquakes. But all these things are merely the beginning of birth pangs."

JESUS

Matthew 24:7,8

"The East Wind is prevailing over the West Wind and war will not break out."

MAO

Speech at the Moscow Meeting of Communist and Workers' Parties (November 18, 1957), quoted in Statement by the Spokesman of the Chinese Government (September 1, 1963).

"You will be hearing of wars and rumors of wars; see that you are not frightened, for those things must take place, but that is not yet the end."

JESUS

Matthew 24:6

"The world is progressing, the future is bright and no one can change this general trend of history."

MAO

On the Chungking Negotiations
(October 17, 1945), **Selected Works,**
Vol. IV, p. 59.

"Because lawlessness is increased, most people's love will grow cold. Then there will be a great tribulation, such as has not occurred since the beginning of the world until now, nor ever shall."

JESUS

Matthew 24:12,21

"U.S. imperialism has not yet been overthrown and it has the atom bomb. I believe it also will be overthrown. It, too, is a paper tiger."

MAO

Speech at the Moscow Meeting of Communist and Workers' Parties (November 18, 1957).

"Do not fear those who kill the body, but are unable to kill the soul; but rather fear Him who is able to destroy both soul and body in hell."

JESUS

Matthew 10:28

"If (the Kuomintang) attack and we wipe them out, they will have that satisfaction; wipe out some, some satisfaction; wipe out more, more satisfaction; wipe out the whole lot, complete satisfaction."

MAO

On the Chungking Negotiations
(October 17, 1945), **Selected Works,**
Vol. IV, p. 56.

"Love your enemies, do good to those who hate you, bless those who curse you, pray for those who mistreat you."

JESUS

Luke 6:27,28

"Only by destroying the enemy in large numbers can one effectively preserve oneself."

MAO

On Protracted War (May 1938), **Selected Works,** Vol. II, p. 156.

"Whoever wishes to save his life shall lose it, but whoever loses his life for My sake, he is the one who will save it."

JESUS

Luke 9:24

"Holding or seizing a city or place is the outcome of wiping out the enemy's effective strength."

MAO

The Present Situation and Our Tasks (December 25, 1947), **Selected Military Writings,** 2nd ed., pp. 349-50.

"Apart from Me you can do nothing."

JESUS

John 15:5

"We should go to the masses and learn from them, synthesize their experience into better, articulated principles and methods, then do propaganda among the masses, and call upon them to put these principles and methods into practice so as to solve their problems and help them achieve liberation and happiness."

MAO

Get Organized (November 29, 1943),
Selected Works, Vol. III, p. 158.

"Go into all the world and preach the gospel to all creation."

JESUS

Mark 16:15

"Our principle is that the Party commands the gun, and the gun must never be allowed to command the Party."

MAO

Problems of War and Strategy
(November 6, 1938), **Selected Works,**
Vol. II, p. 224.

"This is My commandment, that
you love one another, just as I have
loved you."

JESUS

John 15:12

47

"All our officers and fighters must always bear in mind that we are the great People's Liberation Army, we are the troops led by the great Communist Party of China. Provided we constantly observe the directives of the Party, we are sure to win."

MAO

Manifesto of the Chinese People's Liberation Army (October 1947), **Selected Works,** Vol. IV, p. 152.

"In Me you . . . have peace. In the world you have tribulation, but take courage; I have overcome the world."

JESUS

John 16:33

"To lead means not only to decide general and specific policies but also to devise correct methods of work."

MAO

Methods of Work of Party Committees (March 13, 1949), **Selected Works,** Vol. IV, p. 377.

"This is the work of God, that you believe in Him whom He has sent."

JESUS

John 6:29

"Do not talk behind people's backs. Whenever problems arise, call a meeting, place the problems on the table for discussion, take some decisions and the problems will be solved."

MAO

Methods of Work of Party Committees (March 13, 1949), **Selected Works,** Vol. IV, pp. 377-78.

"Whatever you have said in the dark shall be heard in the light, and what you have whispered in the inner rooms shall be proclaimed upon the housetops."

JESUS

Luke 12:3

"Pay attention to uniting and working with comrades who differ with you. This should be borne in mind both in the localities and in the army."

MAO

Methods of Work of Party Committees (March 13, 1949), **Selected Works,** Vol. IV, p. 80.

"If two of you agree on earth about anything that they may ask, it shall be done for them by My Father who is in heaven."

JESUS

Matthew 18:19

"In the appraisal of our work, it is one-sided to regard everything either as all positive or as all negative . . ."

MAO

Speech at the Chinese Communist Party's National Conference on Propaganda Work (March 12, 1957), 1st pocket ed., pp. 16-17.

*"You cannot serve God
and Mammon."*

JESUS

Luke 16:13

"Be united, alert, earnest and lively."

MAO

Motto for the Anti-Japanese Military
and Political College

"You are to be perfect, as your heavenly Father is perfect."

JESUS

Matthew 5:48

"First, we must be ruthless to our enemies, we must overpower and annihilate them. Second, we must be kind to our own, to the people, to our comrades and to our superiors and subordinates, and unite with them."

MAO

Speech at the reception given by the Central Committee of the Party for model study delegates from the Rear Army Detachments (September 18, 1944).

"You have heard that it was said, 'You shall love your neighbor, and hate your enemy.' But I say to you, love your enemies, and pray for those who persecute you."

JESUS

Matthew 5:43,44

"Our slogan in training troops is, 'Officers teach soldiers, soldiers teach officers and soldiers teach each other.'"

MAO

A Talk to the Editorial Staff of the
Shansi-Suiyuan Daily (April 2, 1948),
Selected Works, Vol. IV, p. 243.

"You call me Teacher, and Lord; and you are right; for so I am."

JESUS

John 13:13

"We should be modest and prudent, guard against arrogance and rashness, and serve the Chinese people heart and soul . . ."

MAO

China's Two Possible Destinies (April 23, 1945, **Selected Works,** Vol. III, p. 253.

*"'You shall love the Lord your God
with all your heart, and with all
your soul, and with all your mind.'"*

JESUS

Matthew 22:37

"Our duty is to hold ourselves responsible to the people."

MAO

The Situation and Our Policy after the Victory in the War of Resistance Against Japan (August 13, 1945), **Selected Works,** Vol. IV, p. 16.

*"He who sent Me is with Me . . .
I always do the things that are
pleasing to Him."*

JESUS

John 8:29

"You are respected by all, and quite rightly, but this easily leads to conceit."

MAO

We Must Learn to Do Economic Work (January 10, 1945), **Selected Works,** Vol. III, p. 239.

"Woe to you when all men speak well of you."

JESUS

Luke 6:26

"On what basis should our policy rest? It should rest on our own strength, and that means regeneration through one's own efforts."

MAO

The Situation and Our Policy after the Victory in the War of Resistance Against Japan (August 13, 1945), **Selected Works,** Vol. IV, p. 20.

"Truly, I say to you, unless one is born again, he cannot see the kingdom of God."

JESUS

John 3:3

"We Communists are like seeds and
the people are like the soil. Wherever
we go, we must unite with the
people, take root and blossom
among them."

MAO

On the Chungking Negotiations
(October 17, 1945), **Selected Works,**
Vol. IV, p. 58.

"You shall receive power when the Holy Spirit has come upon you; and you shall be My witnesses both in Jerusalem, and in all Judea and Samaria, and even to the remotest part of the earth."

JESUS

Acts 1:8

"The principle of diligence and frugality should be observed in everything. This principle of economy is one of the basic principles of socialist economics."

MAO

Introductory note to Running a Co-operative Diligently and Frugally (1955), **The Socialist Upsurge in China's Countryside,** Chinese ed., Vol. I.

"I tell you, that to everyone who has shall more be given, but from the one who does not have, even what he does have shall be taken away."

JESUS

Luke 19:26

"We stand for self-reliance . . . We depend on our own efforts, on the creative power of the whole army and the entire people."

MAO

We Must Learn to Do Economic Work (January 10, 1945), **Selected Works,** Vol. III, p. 241.

"I am the vine, you are the branches; he who abides in Me, and I in him, he bears much fruit; for apart from Me you can do nothing."

JESUS

John 15:5

"The wealth of society is created by the workers, peasants and working intellectuals. If they take their destiny into their own hands, follow a Marxist-Leninist line and take an active attitude in solving problems instead of evading them, there will be no difficulty in the world which they cannot overcome."

MAO

Introductory note to The Party Secretary Takes the Lead and All the Party Members Help Run the Co-operatives (1955), **The Socialist Upsurge in China's Countryside,** Chinese ed., Vol. I.

"If you then, being evil, know how to give good gifts to your children, how much more shall your Father who is in heaven give what is good to those who ask Him!"

JESUS

Matthew 7:11

✓ "The history of mankind is one of continuous development from the realm of necessity to the realm of freedom. This process is never-ending."

MAO

Quoted in Premier Chou En-lai's Report on the Work of the Government to the First Session of the Third National Republic of China
(December 21-22, 1964).

"If therefore the Son shall make you free, you shall be free indeed."

JESUS

John 8:36

"Where do correct ideas come from?
Do they drop from the skies? No.
Are they innate in the minds? No.
They come from social practice, and
from it alone."

MAO

Where Do Correct Ideas Come From?
(May 1963), 1st pocket ed., p. 1.

"But the . . . Holy Spirit, whom the Father will send in My name, He will teach you all things, and bring to your remembrance all that I said to you."

JESUS

John 14:26

√ "At first, knowledge is perceptual. The leap to conceptual knowledge, **i.e.,** to ideas, occurs when sufficient perceptual knowledge is accumulated. This is one process in cognition. It is the first stage in the whole process of cognition."

MAO

Where Do Correct Ideas Come From? (May 1963), 1st pocket ed., pp. 1-3.

"If you were blind, you would have no sin; but now you say, 'We see;' your sin remains."

JESUS

John 9:41

"Often, correct knowledge can be arrived at only after many repetitions of the process leading from matter to consciousness and then back to matter, that is, leading from practice to knowledge and then back to practice. Such is the Marxist theory of knowledge, the dialectical materialist theory of knowledge."

MAO

Where Do Correct Ideas Come From?
(May 1963), 1st pocket ed., p. 3.

"When He, the Spirit of truth, comes, He will guide you into all the truth."

JESUS

John 16:13

✓ "All genuine knowledge originates in direct experience."

MAO

On Practice (July 1937), **Selected Works,** Vol. I, pp. 299-300.

"Learn from Me."

JESUS

Matthew 11:29

"'Facts' are all the things that exist objectively, 'truth' means their internal relations, that is, the laws governing them, and 'to seek' means to study."

MAO

Reform Our Study (May 1941), **Selected Works,** Vol. III, pp. 22-23.

"I am the way, and the truth, and the life; no one comes to the Father, but through Me."

JESUS

John 14:6

"It (materialist dialectics) holds that external causes are the basis of change, and that external causes become operative through internal causes. In a suitable temperature an egg changes into a chicken, but no temperature can change a stone into a chicken, because each has a different basis."

MAO

On Contradiction (August 1937), **Selected Works,** Vol. I, p. 314.

"You will know them by their fruits. Grapes are not gathered from thornbushes, nor figs from thistles, are they?"

JESUS

Matthew 7:16

"In this world, things are complicated and are decided by many factors. We should look at problems from different aspects, not from just one."

MAO

On the Chungking Negotiations (October 17, 1945), **Selected Works,** Vol. IV, p. 54.

"Do not judge according to appearance, but judge with righteous judgment."

JESUS

John 7:24

"We must learn to look at problems all-sidedly, seeing the reverse as well as the obverse side of things. In given conditions, a bad thing can lead to good results and a good thing to bad results."

MAO

On the Correct Handling of Contradictions Among the People
(February 27, 1957), 1st pocket ed., pp. 66-67.

"You people judge according to the flesh; I am not judging any one. But even if I do judge, My judgment is true; for I am not alone in it, but I and He who sent me."

JESUS

John 8:15,16

"When Sun Wu Tzu said in discussing military science, 'Know the enemy and know yourself, and you can fight a hundred battles with no danger of defeat,' he was referring to the two sides in a battle. Wei Cheng of the Tang Dynasty also understood the error of one-sidedness when he said, 'Listen to both sides and you will be enlightened, heed only one side and you will be benighted."

MAO

On Contradiction (August 1937), **Selected Works,** Vol. I, pp. 323-24.

"Every one who hears these words of Mine, and acts upon them, may be compared to a wise man."

JESUS

Matthew 7:24

"The stage of action for commanders in a war must be built upon objective possibilities, but on that stage they can direct the performance of many a drama, full of sound and colour, power and grandeur."

MAO

On Protracted War (May 1938), **Selected Works,** Vol. II, p. 152.

"Then the sign of the Son of Man will appear in the sky, and then all the tribes of the earth will mourn, and they will see the Son of Man coming on the clouds of the sky with power and great glory."

JESUS

Matthew 24:30

"Much thinking yields wisdom."

MAO

Our Study and the Current Situation
(April 12, 1944), **Selected Works,**
Vol. III, pp. 174-75.

"Without investigation there cannot
possibly be any right to speak."

MAO

Preface and Postscript to **Rural Surveys**
(March and April 1941), **Selected Works,**
Vol. III, p. 13.

"I will give you utterance and wisdom which none of your opponents will be able to resist or refute."

JESUS

Luke 21:15

"Truly, truly, I say to you, we speak that which we know, and bear witness of that which we have seen."

JESUS

John 3:11

"Modesty helps one to go forward,
whereas conceit makes one
lag behind."

MAO

Opening Address at the Eighth National
Congress of the Communist Party of
China (September 15, 1956).

"Whoever exalts himself shall be
humbled; and whoever humbles
himself shall be exalted."

JESUS

Matthew 23:12

"It is only through the unity of the
Communist Party that the unity of
the whole class and the whole nation
can be achieved, and it is only
through the unity of the whole class
and the whole nation that the enemy
can be defeated and the national
and democratic revolution
accomplished."

MAO

Win the Masses in Their Millions for the
    Anti-Japanese National United Front
(May 7, 1937), **Selected Works,** Vol. I,
p. 292.

"I do not ask in behalf of these alone, but for those also who believe in Me through their word; that they may all be one; even as Thou, Father, art in Me, and I in Thee, that they also may be in Us; that the world may believe that Thou didst send Me."

JESUS

John 17:20,21

✔ "The individual is subordinate to
the organization; the minority is
subordinate to the majority; the
lower level is subordinate to the
higher level."

MAO

The Role of the Chinese Communist
Party in the National War (October
1938), **Selected Works,** Vol. II, pp. 203-4.

"Whoever wishes to be first among you shall be your slave."

JESUS

Matthew 20:27

"As long as we rely on the people, believe firmly in the inexhaustible creative power of the masses and hence trust and identify ourselves with them, we can surmount any difficulty, and no enemy can crush us while we can crush any enemy."

MAO

On Coalition Government (April 24, 1945), **Selected Works,** Vol. III, p. 316.

"He who speaks from himself seeks his own glory; but He who is seeking the glory of the one who sent Him, He is true, and there is no unrighteousness in Him."

JESUS

John 7:18

"The people, and the people alone, are the motive force in the making of world history."

MAO

On Coalition Government (April 24, 1945), **Selected Works,** Vol. III, p. 257.

"Blessed are the gentle, for they shall inherit the earth."

JESUS

Matthew 5:5

"The present upsurge of the peasant movement is a colossal event. In a very short time, in China's central, southern and northern provinces, several hundred million peasants will rise like a mighty storm, like a hurricane, a force so swift and violent that no power, however great, will be able to hold it back. They will smash all the trammels that blind them and rush forward along the road to liberation."

MAO

Report on an Investigation of the Peasant Movement in Hunan (March 1927), **Selected Works,** Vol. I, pp. 23-24.

"These things they will do, because they have not known the Father, or Me."

JESUS

John 16:3

"He who is not afraid of death by a thousand cuts dares to unhorse the emperor — this is the indomitable spirit needed in our struggle to build socialism and communism."

MAO

Speech at the Chinese Communist Party's National Conference on Propaganda Work (March 12, 1957), 1st pocket ed., p. 16.

"But seek first His Kingdom, and His righteousness; and all these things shall be added to you."

JESUS

Matthew 6:33

∨ "A Communist . . . should be more concerned about the Party and the masses than about any individual, and more concerned about others than about himself. Only thus can he be considered a Communist."

MAO

Combat Liberalism (September 7, 1937), **Selected Works,** Vol. II, p. 33.

"He who does not take his cross and follow after Me is not worthy of Me."

JESUS

Matthew 10:38

"Communists must be ready at all times to stand up for the truth, because truth is in the interests of the people; Communists must be ready at all times to correct their mistakes, because mistakes are against the interests of the people."

MAO

On Coalition Government (April 24, 1945), **Selected Works,** Vol. III, p. 315.

"You shall know the truth, and the truth shall make you free."

JESUS

John 8:32

"Communists must always go into the whys and wherefores of anything, use their own heads and carefully think over whether or not it corresponds to reality and is really well founded."

MAO

Rectify the Party's Style of Work (February 1, 1942), **Selected Works,** Vol. III, pp. 49-50.

"False Christs and false prophets will arise and will show great signs and wonders, so as to mislead, if possible, even the elect. Behold, I have told you in advance."

JESUS

Matthew 24:24,25

"We are not only good at destroying the old world, we are also good at building the new."

MAO

Report to the Second Plenary Session of the Seventh Central Committee of the Communist Party of China (March 5, 1949), **Selected Works,** Vol. IV, p. 374.

"Behold, I am making all things new."

JESUS

Revelation 21:5

"We the Chinese nation have the spirit to fight the enemy to the last drop of our blood, the determination to recover our lost territory by our own efforts, and the ability to stand on our own feet in the family of nations."

MAO

On Tactics Against Japanese Imperialism (December 27, 1935), **Selected Works,** Vol. I, p. 170.

"All things have been handed over to Me by My Father."

JESUS

Matthew 11:27